THIS GARDEN PLANNER JOURNAL

BELONGS TO:

D1039124

CONTENTS

LIST OF PLANTS TO TRY

WARM - SEASON

- [ ]
- [ ]
- [ ]
- [ ]
- [ ]
- [ ]
- [ ]
- [ ]
- [ ]
- [ ]
- [ ]
- [ ]
- [ ]
- [ ]

COOL - SEASON

- [ ]
- [ ]
- [ ]
- [ ]
- [ ]
- [ ]
- [ ]
- [ ]
- [ ]
- [ ]
- [ ]
- [ ]
- [ ]
- [ ]

PLANTING HARDINESS ZONE:

LAST FROST DATE:

FIRST FROST DATE:

 **LIST OF PLANTS TO TRY**   **YEAR:**

WARM - SEASON	**COOL - SEASON**
☐	☐
☐	☐
☐	☐
☐	☐
☐	☐
☐	☐
☐	☐
☐	☐
☐	☐
☐	☐
☐	☐
☐	☐
☐	☐
☐	☐

PLANTING HARDINESS ZONE:

LAST FROST DATE:

FIRST FROST DATE:

NOTES:

GARDEN LAYOUT #2

NOTES:

_____

_____

_____

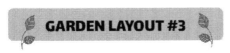

NOTES:

GARDEN LAYOUT #4

NOTES:
_____

_____

_____

SEEDS AND TRANSPLANTS

SEEDS	DATE PLANTED

TRANSPLANTS	DATE PLANTED

SEEDS AND TRANSPLANTS

SEEDS	DATE PLANTED

TRANSPLANTS	DATE PLANTED

SEEDS AND TRANSPLANTS

SEEDS	DATE PLANTED

TRANSPLANTS	DATE PLANTED

SEEDS AND TRANSPLANTS

SEEDS	DATE PLANTED

TRANSPLANTS	DATE PLANTED

IMPORTANT TASKS

TASK	S	M	T	W	TH	F	S
_____	☐	☐	☐	☐	☐	☐	☐
_____	☐	☐	☐	☐	☐	☐	☐
_____	☐	☐	☐	☐	☐	☐	☐
_____	☐	☐	☐	☐	☐	☐	☐
_____	☐	☐	☐	☐	☐	☐	☐
_____	☐	☐	☐	☐	☐	☐	☐
_____	☐	☐	☐	☐	☐	☐	☐
_____	☐	☐	☐	☐	☐	☐	☐
_____	☐	☐	☐	☐	☐	☐	☐
_____	☐	☐	☐	☐	☐	☐	☐
_____	☐	☐	☐	☐	☐	☐	☐
_____	☐	☐	☐	☐	☐	☐	☐
_____	☐	☐	☐	☐	☐	☐	☐

NOTES:
_____
_____
_____
_____

PLANT INFORMATION

PLANT NAME: _____   TYPE/VARIETY: _____

SEED ☐   TRANSPLANT ☐   DATE PLANTED: _____

SUNLIGHT EXPOSURE: SUCCESSION PLANT DATE: _____

FULL SUN ☐   PART SHADE ☐   SUCCESSION PLANT DATE: _____

PART SUN ☐   FULL SHADE ☐   SUCCESSION PLANT DATE: _____

BLOOMING DATE: DATE OF FIRST HARVEST:

HOW MUCH WATER DOES THIS PLANT NEED? _____

_____

_____

_____

HOW MUCH AND WHAT TYPE OF FERTILIZER DOES THIS PLANT NEED? _____

_____

_____

_____

WHAT PESTS OR DISEASES AFFECT THIS PLANT? _____

_____

_____

_____

_____

WHAT INSECTICIDE OR BARRIER WAS USED AND WHAT WERE THE RESULTS?

_____

_____

_____

_____

_____

WHAT FERTILIZER WAS USED, WHEN WAS IT USED AND WHAT WERE THE
RESULTS? _____

_____

_____

_____

_____

HOW MUCH WAS THE HARVEST? _____

_____

_____

_____

_____

IMPORTANT TASKS/NOTES:
_____

_____

_____

_____

PLANT INFORMATION

PLANT NAME: _____   TYPE/VARIETY: _____

SEED ☐   TRANSPLANT ☐   DATE PLANTED: _____

SUNLIGHT EXPOSURE: SUCCESSION PLANT DATE: _____

FULL SUN ☐   PART SHADE ☐   SUCCESSION PLANT DATE: _____

PART SUN ☐   FULL SHADE ☐   SUCCESSION PLANT DATE: _____

BLOOMING DATE: DATE OF FIRST HARVEST:

HOW MUCH WATER DOES THIS PLANT NEED? _____

_____

_____

_____

HOW MUCH AND WHAT TYPE OF FERTILIZER DOES THIS PLANT NEED? _____

_____

_____

_____

WHAT PESTS OR DISEASES AFFECT THIS PLANT? _____

_____

_____

_____

_____

WHAT INSECTICIDE OR BARRIER WAS USED AND WHAT WERE THE RESULTS?

_____

_____

_____

_____

_____

WHAT FERTILIZER WAS USED, WHEN WAS IT USED AND WHAT WERE THE
RESULTS? _____

_____

_____

_____

_____

HOW MUCH WAS THE HARVEST? _____

_____

_____

_____

_____

IMPORTANT TASKS/NOTES:
_____

_____

_____

_____

PLANT INFORMATION

PLANT NAME: _____   TYPE/VARIETY: _____

SEED ☐   TRANSPLANT ☐   DATE PLANTED: _____

SUNLIGHT EXPOSURE: SUCCESSION PLANT DATE: _____

FULL SUN ☐   PART SHADE ☐   SUCCESSION PLANT DATE: _____

PART SUN ☐   FULL SHADE ☐   SUCCESSION PLANT DATE: _____

BLOOMING DATE: DATE OF FIRST HARVEST:

HOW MUCH WATER DOES THIS PLANT NEED? _____

_____

_____

_____

HOW MUCH AND WHAT TYPE OF FERTILIZER DOES THIS PLANT NEED? _____

_____

_____

_____

WHAT PESTS OR DISEASES AFFECT THIS PLANT? _____

_____

_____

_____

_____

WHAT INSECTICIDE OR BARRIER WAS USED AND WHAT WERE THE RESULTS?

_____

_____

_____

_____

_____

WHAT FERTILIZER WAS USED, WHEN WAS IT USED AND WHAT WERE THE
RESULTS? _____

_____

_____

_____

_____

HOW MUCH WAS THE HARVEST? _____

_____

_____

_____

_____

IMPORTANT TASKS/NOTES:

_____

_____

_____

_____

PLANT INFORMATION

PLANT NAME: _____ TYPE/VARIETY: _____

SEED ☐ TRANSPLANT ☐ DATE PLANTED: _____

SUNLIGHT EXPOSURE: SUCCESSION PLANT DATE: _____

FULL SUN ☐ PART SHADE ☐ SUCCESSION PLANT DATE: _____

PART SUN ☐ FULL SHADE ☐ SUCCESSION PLANT DATE: _____

BLOOMING DATE: DATE OF FIRST HARVEST:

HOW MUCH WATER DOES THIS PLANT NEED? _____

_____

_____

_____

HOW MUCH AND WHAT TYPE OF FERTILIZER DOES THIS PLANT NEED? _____

_____

_____

_____

WHAT PESTS OR DISEASES AFFECT THIS PLANT? _____

_____

_____

_____

_____

WHAT INSECTICIDE OR BARRIER WAS USED AND WHAT WERE THE RESULTS?

_____

_____

_____

_____

_____

WHAT FERTILIZER WAS USED, WHEN WAS IT USED AND WHAT WERE THE
RESULTS? _____

_____

_____

_____

_____

HOW MUCH WAS THE HARVEST? _____

_____

_____

_____

_____

IMPORTANT TASKS/NOTES:
_____

_____

_____

_____

PLANT INFORMATION

PLANT NAME: _____ TYPE/VARIETY: _____

SEED ☐ TRANSPLANT ☐ DATE PLANTED: _____

SUNLIGHT EXPOSURE: SUCCESSION PLANT DATE: _____

FULL SUN ☐ PART SHADE ☐ SUCCESSION PLANT DATE: _____

PART SUN ☐ FULL SHADE ☐ SUCCESSION PLANT DATE: _____

BLOOMING DATE: DATE OF FIRST HARVEST:

HOW MUCH WATER DOES THIS PLANT NEED? _____

_____

_____

_____

HOW MUCH AND WHAT TYPE OF FERTILIZER DOES THIS PLANT NEED? _____

_____

_____

_____

WHAT PESTS OR DISEASES AFFECT THIS PLANT? _____

_____

_____

_____

_____

WHAT INSECTICIDE OR BARRIER WAS USED AND WHAT WERE THE RESULTS?

_____

_____

_____

_____

WHAT FERTILIZER WAS USED, WHEN WAS IT USED AND WHAT WERE THE
RESULTS? _____

_____

_____

_____

_____

HOW MUCH WAS THE HARVEST? _____

_____

_____

_____

_____

IMPORTANT TASKS/NOTES:
_____

_____

_____

_____

PLANT INFORMATION

PLANT NAME: _____   TYPE/VARIETY: _____

SEED ☐   TRANSPLANT ☐   DATE PLANTED: _____

SUNLIGHT EXPOSURE: SUCCESSION PLANT DATE: _____

FULL SUN ☐   PART SHADE ☐   SUCCESSION PLANT DATE: _____

PART SUN ☐   FULL SHADE ☐   SUCCESSION PLANT DATE: _____

BLOOMING DATE: DATE OF FIRST HARVEST:

HOW MUCH WATER DOES THIS PLANT NEED? _____

_____

_____

_____

HOW MUCH AND WHAT TYPE OF FERTILIZER DOES THIS PLANT NEED? _____

_____

_____

_____

WHAT PESTS OR DISEASES AFFECT THIS PLANT? _____

_____

_____

_____

_____

WHAT INSECTICIDE OR BARRIER WAS USED AND WHAT WERE THE RESULTS?

_____

_____

_____

_____

_____

WHAT FERTILIZER WAS USED, WHEN WAS IT USED AND WHAT WERE THE
RESULTS? _____

_____

_____

_____

_____

HOW MUCH WAS THE HARVEST? _____

_____

_____

_____

_____

IMPORTANT TASKS/NOTES:
_____

_____

_____

_____

PLANT INFORMATION

PLANT NAME: _____   TYPE/VARIETY: _____

SEED ☐   TRANSPLANT ☐   DATE PLANTED: _____

SUNLIGHT EXPOSURE: SUCCESSION PLANT DATE: _____

FULL SUN ☐   PART SHADE ☐   SUCCESSION PLANT DATE: _____

PART SUN ☐   FULL SHADE ☐   SUCCESSION PLANT DATE: _____

BLOOMING DATE: DATE OF FIRST HARVEST:

HOW MUCH WATER DOES THIS PLANT NEED? _____

_____

_____

_____

HOW MUCH AND WHAT TYPE OF FERTILIZER DOES THIS PLANT NEED? _____

_____

_____

_____

WHAT PESTS OR DISEASES AFFECT THIS PLANT? _____

_____

_____

_____

_____

WHAT INSECTICIDE OR BARRIER WAS USED AND WHAT WERE THE RESULTS?

_____

_____

_____

_____

_____

WHAT FERTILIZER WAS USED, WHEN WAS IT USED AND WHAT WERE THE
RESULTS? _____

_____

_____

_____

_____

HOW MUCH WAS THE HARVEST? _____

_____

_____

_____

_____

IMPORTANT TASKS/NOTES:
_____

_____

_____

_____

PLANT INFORMATION

PLANT NAME: _____   TYPE/VARIETY: _____

SEED ☐   TRANSPLANT ☐   DATE PLANTED: _____

SUNLIGHT EXPOSURE: SUCCESSION PLANT DATE: _____

FULL SUN ☐   PART SHADE ☐   SUCCESSION PLANT DATE: _____

PART SUN ☐   FULL SHADE ☐   SUCCESSION PLANT DATE: _____

BLOOMING DATE: DATE OF FIRST HARVEST:

HOW MUCH WATER DOES THIS PLANT NEED? _____

_____

_____

_____

HOW MUCH AND WHAT TYPE OF FERTILIZER DOES THIS PLANT NEED? _____

_____

_____

_____

WHAT PESTS OR DISEASES AFFECT THIS PLANT? _____

_____

_____

_____

_____

WHAT INSECTICIDE OR BARRIER WAS USED AND WHAT WERE THE RESULTS?

_____

_____

_____

_____

_____

WHAT FERTILIZER WAS USED, WHEN WAS IT USED AND WHAT WERE THE
RESULTS? _____

_____

_____

_____

_____

HOW MUCH WAS THE HARVEST? _____

_____

_____

_____

_____

IMPORTANT TASKS/NOTES:
_____

_____

_____

_____

PLANT INFORMATION

PLANT NAME: _____   TYPE/VARIETY: _____

SEED ☐   TRANSPLANT ☐   DATE PLANTED: _____

SUNLIGHT EXPOSURE: SUCCESSION PLANT DATE: _____

FULL SUN ☐   PART SHADE ☐   SUCCESSION PLANT DATE: _____

PART SUN ☐   FULL SHADE ☐   SUCCESSION PLANT DATE: _____

BLOOMING DATE: DATE OF FIRST HARVEST:

HOW MUCH WATER DOES THIS PLANT NEED? _____

_____

_____

_____

HOW MUCH AND WHAT TYPE OF FERTILIZER DOES THIS PLANT NEED? _____

_____

_____

_____

WHAT PESTS OR DISEASES AFFECT THIS PLANT? _____

_____

_____

_____

_____

WHAT INSECTICIDE OR BARRIER WAS USED AND WHAT WERE THE RESULTS?

_____

_____

_____

_____

WHAT FERTILIZER WAS USED, WHEN WAS IT USED AND WHAT WERE THE
RESULTS? _____

_____

_____

_____

HOW MUCH WAS THE HARVEST? _____

_____

_____

_____

_____

IMPORTANT TASKS/NOTES:
_____

_____

_____

_____

PLANT INFORMATION

PLANT NAME: _____   TYPE/VARIETY: _____

SEED ☐   TRANSPLANT ☐   DATE PLANTED: _____

SUNLIGHT EXPOSURE: SUCCESSION PLANT DATE: _____

FULL SUN ☐   PART SHADE ☐   SUCCESSION PLANT DATE: _____

PART SUN ☐   FULL SHADE ☐   SUCCESSION PLANT DATE: _____

BLOOMING DATE: DATE OF FIRST HARVEST:

HOW MUCH WATER DOES THIS PLANT NEED? _____

_____

_____

_____

HOW MUCH AND WHAT TYPE OF FERTILIZER DOES THIS PLANT NEED? _____

_____

_____

_____

WHAT PESTS OR DISEASES AFFECT THIS PLANT? _____

_____

_____

_____

_____

WHAT INSECTICIDE OR BARRIER WAS USED AND WHAT WERE THE RESULTS?

_____

_____

_____

_____

_____

WHAT FERTILIZER WAS USED, WHEN WAS IT USED AND WHAT WERE THE
RESULTS? _____

_____

_____

_____

_____

HOW MUCH WAS THE HARVEST? _____

_____

_____

_____

_____

IMPORTANT TASKS/NOTES:
_____

_____

_____

_____

PLANT INFORMATION

PLANT NAME: _____   TYPE/VARIETY: _____

SEED ☐   TRANSPLANT ☐   DATE PLANTED: _____

SUNLIGHT EXPOSURE: SUCCESSION PLANT DATE: _____

FULL SUN ☐   PART SHADE ☐   SUCCESSION PLANT DATE: _____

PART SUN ☐   FULL SHADE ☐   SUCCESSION PLANT DATE: _____

BLOOMING DATE: DATE OF FIRST HARVEST:

HOW MUCH WATER DOES THIS PLANT NEED? _____

_____

_____

_____

HOW MUCH AND WHAT TYPE OF FERTILIZER DOES THIS PLANT NEED? _____

_____

_____

_____

WHAT PESTS OR DISEASES AFFECT THIS PLANT? _____

_____

_____

_____

_____

WHAT INSECTICIDE OR BARRIER WAS USED AND WHAT WERE THE RESULTS?

_____
_____
_____
_____

WHAT FERTILIZER WAS USED, WHEN WAS IT USED AND WHAT WERE THE
RESULTS? _____

_____
_____
_____
_____

HOW MUCH WAS THE HARVEST? _____

_____
_____
_____
_____

IMPORTANT TASKS/NOTES: _____

_____
_____
_____

PLANT INFORMATION

PLANT NAME: _____   TYPE/VARIETY: _____

SEED ☐   TRANSPLANT ☐   DATE PLANTED: _____

SUNLIGHT EXPOSURE: SUCCESSION PLANT DATE: _____

FULL SUN ☐   PART SHADE ☐   SUCCESSION PLANT DATE: _____

PART SUN ☐   FULL SHADE ☐   SUCCESSION PLANT DATE: _____

BLOOMING DATE: DATE OF FIRST HARVEST:

HOW MUCH WATER DOES THIS PLANT NEED? _____

_____

_____

_____

HOW MUCH AND WHAT TYPE OF FERTILIZER DOES THIS PLANT NEED? _____

_____

_____

_____

WHAT PESTS OR DISEASES AFFECT THIS PLANT? _____

_____

_____

_____

_____

WHAT INSECTICIDE OR BARRIER WAS USED AND WHAT WERE THE RESULTS?

_____

_____

_____

_____

_____

WHAT FERTILIZER WAS USED, WHEN WAS IT USED AND WHAT WERE THE
RESULTS? _____

_____

_____

_____

_____

HOW MUCH WAS THE HARVEST? _____

_____

_____

_____

_____

IMPORTANT TASKS/NOTES: _____

_____

_____

_____

PLANT INFORMATION

PLANT NAME: _____   TYPE/VARIETY: _____

SEED ☐   TRANSPLANT ☐   DATE PLANTED: _____

SUNLIGHT EXPOSURE: SUCCESSION PLANT DATE: _____

FULL SUN ☐   PART SHADE ☐   SUCCESSION PLANT DATE: _____

PART SUN ☐   FULL SHADE ☐   SUCCESSION PLANT DATE: _____

BLOOMING DATE: DATE OF FIRST HARVEST:

HOW MUCH WATER DOES THIS PLANT NEED? _____

_____

_____

_____

HOW MUCH AND WHAT TYPE OF FERTILIZER DOES THIS PLANT NEED? _____

_____

_____

_____

WHAT PESTS OR DISEASES AFFECT THIS PLANT? _____

_____

_____

_____

_____

WHAT INSECTICIDE OR BARRIER WAS USED AND WHAT WERE THE RESULTS?

_____

_____

_____

_____

_____

WHAT FERTILIZER WAS USED, WHEN WAS IT USED AND WHAT WERE THE
RESULTS? _____

_____

_____

_____

_____

HOW MUCH WAS THE HARVEST? _____

_____

_____

_____

_____

IMPORTANT TASKS/NOTES:
_____

_____

_____

_____

PLANT INFORMATION

PLANT NAME: _____   TYPE/VARIETY: _____

SEED ☐   TRANSPLANT ☐   DATE PLANTED: _____

SUNLIGHT EXPOSURE: SUCCESSION PLANT DATE: _____

FULL SUN ☐   PART SHADE ☐   SUCCESSION PLANT DATE: _____

PART SUN ☐   FULL SHADE ☐   SUCCESSION PLANT DATE: _____

BLOOMING DATE: DATE OF FIRST HARVEST:

HOW MUCH WATER DOES THIS PLANT NEED? _____

_____

_____

_____

HOW MUCH AND WHAT TYPE OF FERTILIZER DOES THIS PLANT NEED? _____

_____

_____

_____

WHAT PESTS OR DISEASES AFFECT THIS PLANT? _____

_____

_____

_____

_____

WHAT INSECTICIDE OR BARRIER WAS USED AND WHAT WERE THE RESULTS?

_____

_____

_____

_____

_____

WHAT FERTILIZER WAS USED, WHEN WAS IT USED AND WHAT WERE THE
RESULTS? _____

_____

_____

_____

_____

HOW MUCH WAS THE HARVEST? _____

_____

_____

_____

_____

IMPORTANT TASKS/NOTES:
_____

_____

_____

_____

PLANT INFORMATION

PLANT NAME: _____   TYPE/VARIETY: _____

SEED ☐   TRANSPLANT ☐   DATE PLANTED: _____

SUNLIGHT EXPOSURE: SUCCESSION PLANT DATE: _____

FULL SUN ☐   PART SHADE ☐   SUCCESSION PLANT DATE: _____

PART SUN ☐   FULL SHADE ☐   SUCCESSION PLANT DATE: _____

BLOOMING DATE: DATE OF FIRST HARVEST:

HOW MUCH WATER DOES THIS PLANT NEED? _____

_____

_____

_____

HOW MUCH AND WHAT TYPE OF FERTILIZER DOES THIS PLANT NEED? _____

_____

_____

_____

WHAT PESTS OR DISEASES AFFECT THIS PLANT? _____

_____

_____

_____

_____

WHAT INSECTICIDE OR BARRIER WAS USED AND WHAT WERE THE RESULTS?

_____

_____

_____

_____

WHAT FERTILIZER WAS USED, WHEN WAS IT USED AND WHAT WERE THE
RESULTS? _____

_____

_____

_____

HOW MUCH WAS THE HARVEST? _____

_____

_____

_____

_____

IMPORTANT TASKS/NOTES:
_____

_____

_____

_____

PLANT INFORMATION

PLANT NAME: _____ TYPE/VARIETY: _____

SEED ☐   TRANSPLANT ☐   DATE PLANTED: _____

SUNLIGHT EXPOSURE:

SUCCESSION PLANT DATE: _____

FULL SUN ☐   PART SHADE ☐   SUCCESSION PLANT DATE: _____

PART SUN ☐   FULL SHADE ☐   SUCCESSION PLANT DATE: _____

BLOOMING DATE: DATE OF FIRST HARVEST:

HOW MUCH WATER DOES THIS PLANT NEED? _____

_____

_____

_____

HOW MUCH AND WHAT TYPE OF FERTILIZER DOES THIS PLANT NEED? _____

_____

_____

_____

WHAT PESTS OR DISEASES AFFECT THIS PLANT? _____

_____

_____

_____

_____

WHAT INSECTICIDE OR BARRIER WAS USED AND WHAT WERE THE RESULTS?

_____

_____

_____

_____

_____

WHAT FERTILIZER WAS USED, WHEN WAS IT USED AND WHAT WERE THE
RESULTS? _____

_____

_____

_____

_____

HOW MUCH WAS THE HARVEST? _____

_____

_____

_____

_____

IMPORTANT TASKS/NOTES:

_____

_____

_____

_____

PLANT INFORMATION

PLANT NAME: _____   TYPE/VARIETY: _____

SEED ☐   TRANSPLANT ☐   DATE PLANTED: _____

SUNLIGHT EXPOSURE: SUCCESSION PLANT DATE: _____

FULL SUN ☐   PART SHADE ☐   SUCCESSION PLANT DATE: _____

PART SUN ☐   FULL SHADE ☐   SUCCESSION PLANT DATE: _____

BLOOMING DATE: DATE OF FIRST HARVEST:

HOW MUCH WATER DOES THIS PLANT NEED? _____

_____

_____

_____

HOW MUCH AND WHAT TYPE OF FERTILIZER DOES THIS PLANT NEED? _____

_____

_____

_____

WHAT PESTS OR DISEASES AFFECT THIS PLANT? _____

_____

_____

_____

_____

WHAT INSECTICIDE OR BARRIER WAS USED AND WHAT WERE THE RESULTS?

_____

_____

_____

_____

_____

WHAT FERTILIZER WAS USED, WHEN WAS IT USED AND WHAT WERE THE
RESULTS? _____

_____

_____

_____

_____

HOW MUCH WAS THE HARVEST? _____

_____

_____

_____

_____

IMPORTANT TASKS/NOTES:
_____

_____

_____

_____

PLANT INFORMATION

PLANT NAME: _____   TYPE/VARIETY: _____

SEED ☐   TRANSPLANT ☐   DATE PLANTED: _____

SUNLIGHT EXPOSURE: SUCCESSION PLANT DATE: _____

FULL SUN ☐   PART SHADE ☐   SUCCESSION PLANT DATE: _____

PART SUN ☐   FULL SHADE ☐   SUCCESSION PLANT DATE: _____

BLOOMING DATE: DATE OF FIRST HARVEST:

HOW MUCH WATER DOES THIS PLANT NEED? _____

_____

_____

_____

HOW MUCH AND WHAT TYPE OF FERTILIZER DOES THIS PLANT NEED? _____

_____

_____

_____

WHAT PESTS OR DISEASES AFFECT THIS PLANT? _____

_____

_____

_____

_____

WHAT INSECTICIDE OR BARRIER WAS USED AND WHAT WERE THE RESULTS?

_____

_____

_____

_____

_____

WHAT FERTILIZER WAS USED, WHEN WAS IT USED AND WHAT WERE THE
RESULTS? _____

_____

_____

_____

_____

HOW MUCH WAS THE HARVEST? _____

_____

_____

_____

_____

IMPORTANT TASKS/NOTES:
_____

_____

_____

_____

PLANT INFORMATION

PLANT NAME: _____   TYPE/VARIETY: _____

SEED ☐   TRANSPLANT ☐   DATE PLANTED: _____

SUNLIGHT EXPOSURE: SUCCESSION PLANT DATE: _____

FULL SUN ☐   PART SHADE ☐   SUCCESSION PLANT DATE: _____

PART SUN ☐   FULL SHADE ☐   SUCCESSION PLANT DATE: _____

BLOOMING DATE: DATE OF FIRST HARVEST:

HOW MUCH WATER DOES THIS PLANT NEED? _____

_____

_____

_____

HOW MUCH AND WHAT TYPE OF FERTILIZER DOES THIS PLANT NEED? _____

_____

_____

_____

WHAT PESTS OR DISEASES AFFECT THIS PLANT? _____

_____

_____

_____

_____

WHAT INSECTICIDE OR BARRIER WAS USED AND WHAT WERE THE RESULTS?

_____

_____

_____

_____

_____

WHAT FERTILIZER WAS USED, WHEN WAS IT USED AND WHAT WERE THE RESULTS? _____

_____

_____

_____

_____

HOW MUCH WAS THE HARVEST? _____

_____

_____

_____

_____

IMPORTANT TASKS/NOTES:
_____

_____

_____

_____

PLANT INFORMATION

PLANT NAME: _____   TYPE/VARIETY: _____

SEED ☐   TRANSPLANT ☐   DATE PLANTED: _____

SUNLIGHT EXPOSURE: SUCCESSION PLANT DATE: _____

FULL SUN ☐   PART SHADE ☐   SUCCESSION PLANT DATE: _____

PART SUN ☐   FULL SHADE ☐   SUCCESSION PLANT DATE: _____

BLOOMING DATE: DATE OF FIRST HARVEST:

HOW MUCH WATER DOES THIS PLANT NEED? _____

_____

_____

_____

HOW MUCH AND WHAT TYPE OF FERTILIZER DOES THIS PLANT NEED? _____

_____

_____

_____

WHAT PESTS OR DISEASES AFFECT THIS PLANT? _____

_____

_____

_____

_____

WHAT INSECTICIDE OR BARRIER WAS USED AND WHAT WERE THE RESULTS?

_____

_____

_____

_____

WHAT FERTILIZER WAS USED, WHEN WAS IT USED AND WHAT WERE THE
RESULTS? _____

_____

_____

_____

_____

HOW MUCH WAS THE HARVEST? _____

_____

_____

_____

_____

IMPORTANT TASKS/NOTES:

_____

_____

_____

_____

PLANT INFORMATION

PLANT NAME: _____   TYPE/VARIETY: _____

SEED ☐   TRANSPLANT ☐   DATE PLANTED: _____

SUNLIGHT EXPOSURE: SUCCESSION PLANT DATE: _____

FULL SUN ☐   PART SHADE ☐   SUCCESSION PLANT DATE: _____

PART SUN ☐   FULL SHADE ☐   SUCCESSION PLANT DATE: _____

BLOOMING DATE: DATE OF FIRST HARVEST:

HOW MUCH WATER DOES THIS PLANT NEED? _____

_____

_____

_____

HOW MUCH AND WHAT TYPE OF FERTILIZER DOES THIS PLANT NEED? _____

_____

_____

_____

WHAT PESTS OR DISEASES AFFECT THIS PLANT? _____

_____

_____

_____

_____

WHAT INSECTICIDE OR BARRIER WAS USED AND WHAT WERE THE RESULTS?

_____

_____

_____

_____

WHAT FERTILIZER WAS USED, WHEN WAS IT USED AND WHAT WERE THE
RESULTS? _____

_____

_____

_____

HOW MUCH WAS THE HARVEST? _____

_____

_____

_____

_____

IMPORTANT TASKS/NOTES:

_____

_____

_____

PLANT INFORMATION

PLANT NAME: _____   TYPE/VARIETY: _____

SEED ☐   TRANSPLANT ☐   DATE PLANTED: _____

SUNLIGHT EXPOSURE: SUCCESSION PLANT DATE: _____

FULL SUN ☐   PART SHADE ☐   SUCCESSION PLANT DATE: _____

PART SUN ☐   FULL SHADE ☐   SUCCESSION PLANT DATE: _____

BLOOMING DATE: DATE OF FIRST HARVEST:

HOW MUCH WATER DOES THIS PLANT NEED? _____

_____

_____

_____

HOW MUCH AND WHAT TYPE OF FERTILIZER DOES THIS PLANT NEED? _____

_____

_____

_____

WHAT PESTS OR DISEASES AFFECT THIS PLANT? _____

_____

_____

_____

_____

WHAT INSECTICIDE OR BARRIER WAS USED AND WHAT WERE THE RESULTS?

_____

_____

_____

_____

WHAT FERTILIZER WAS USED, WHEN WAS IT USED AND WHAT WERE THE
RESULTS? _____

_____

_____

_____

HOW MUCH WAS THE HARVEST? _____

_____

_____

_____

IMPORTANT TASKS/NOTES:

_____

_____

_____

PLANT INFORMATION

PLANT NAME: _____   TYPE/VARIETY: _____

SEED ☐   TRANSPLANT ☐   DATE PLANTED: _____

SUNLIGHT EXPOSURE: SUCCESSION PLANT DATE: _____

FULL SUN ☐   PART SHADE ☐   SUCCESSION PLANT DATE: _____

PART SUN ☐   FULL SHADE ☐   SUCCESSION PLANT DATE: _____

BLOOMING DATE: DATE OF FIRST HARVEST:

HOW MUCH WATER DOES THIS PLANT NEED? _____

_____

_____

_____

HOW MUCH AND WHAT TYPE OF FERTILIZER DOES THIS PLANT NEED? _____

_____

_____

_____

WHAT PESTS OR DISEASES AFFECT THIS PLANT? _____

_____

_____

_____

_____

WHAT INSECTICIDE OR BARRIER WAS USED AND WHAT WERE THE RESULTS?

_____

_____

_____

_____

WHAT FERTILIZER WAS USED, WHEN WAS IT USED AND WHAT WERE THE
RESULTS? _____

_____

_____

_____

_____

HOW MUCH WAS THE HARVEST? _____

_____

_____

_____

_____

IMPORTANT TASKS/NOTES:

_____

_____

_____

PLANT INFORMATION

PLANT NAME: _____   TYPE/VARIETY: _____

SEED ☐   TRANSPLANT ☐   DATE PLANTED: _____

SUNLIGHT EXPOSURE: SUCCESSION PLANT DATE: _____

FULL SUN ☐   PART SHADE ☐   SUCCESSION PLANT DATE: _____

PART SUN ☐   FULL SHADE ☐   SUCCESSION PLANT DATE: _____

BLOOMING DATE: DATE OF FIRST HARVEST:

HOW MUCH WATER DOES THIS PLANT NEED? _____

_____

_____

_____

HOW MUCH AND WHAT TYPE OF FERTILIZER DOES THIS PLANT NEED? _____

_____

_____

_____

WHAT PESTS OR DISEASES AFFECT THIS PLANT? _____

_____

_____

_____

_____

WHAT INSECTICIDE OR BARRIER WAS USED AND WHAT WERE THE RESULTS?

_____

_____

_____

_____

WHAT FERTILIZER WAS USED, WHEN WAS IT USED AND WHAT WERE THE
RESULTS? _____

_____

_____

_____

_____

HOW MUCH WAS THE HARVEST? _____

_____

_____

_____

_____

IMPORTANT TASKS/NOTES:

_____

_____

_____

PLANT INFORMATION

PLANT NAME: _____   TYPE/VARIETY: _____

SEED ☐   TRANSPLANT ☐   DATE PLANTED: _____

SUNLIGHT EXPOSURE: SUCCESSION PLANT DATE: _____

FULL SUN ☐   PART SHADE ☐   SUCCESSION PLANT DATE: _____

PART SUN ☐   FULL SHADE ☐   SUCCESSION PLANT DATE: _____

BLOOMING DATE: DATE OF FIRST HARVEST:

HOW MUCH WATER DOES THIS PLANT NEED? _____

_____

_____

_____

HOW MUCH AND WHAT TYPE OF FERTILIZER DOES THIS PLANT NEED? _____

_____

_____

_____

WHAT PESTS OR DISEASES AFFECT THIS PLANT? _____

_____

_____

_____

_____

WHAT INSECTICIDE OR BARRIER WAS USED AND WHAT WERE THE RESULTS?

_____

_____

_____

_____

WHAT FERTILIZER WAS USED, WHEN WAS IT USED AND WHAT WERE THE
RESULTS? _____

_____

_____

_____

_____

HOW MUCH WAS THE HARVEST? _____

_____

_____

_____

_____

IMPORTANT TASKS/NOTES:

_____

_____

_____

PLANT INFORMATION

PLANT NAME: _____   TYPE/VARIETY: _____

SEED ☐   TRANSPLANT ☐   DATE PLANTED: _____

SUNLIGHT EXPOSURE: _____   SUCCESSION PLANT DATE: _____

FULL SUN ☐   PART SHADE ☐   SUCCESSION PLANT DATE: _____

PART SUN ☐   FULL SHADE ☐   SUCCESSION PLANT DATE: _____

BLOOMING DATE: DATE OF FIRST HARVEST:

HOW MUCH WATER DOES THIS PLANT NEED? _____

_____

_____

_____

HOW MUCH AND WHAT TYPE OF FERTILIZER DOES THIS PLANT NEED? _____

_____

_____

_____

WHAT PESTS OR DISEASES AFFECT THIS PLANT? _____

_____

_____

_____

_____

WHAT INSECTICIDE OR BARRIER WAS USED AND WHAT WERE THE RESULTS?

_____

_____

_____

_____

_____

WHAT FERTILIZER WAS USED, WHEN WAS IT USED AND WHAT WERE THE
RESULTS? _____

_____

_____

_____

_____

HOW MUCH WAS THE HARVEST? _____

_____

_____

_____

_____

IMPORTANT TASKS/NOTES:

_____

_____

_____

_____

PLANT INFORMATION

PLANT NAME: _____   TYPE/VARIETY: _____

SEED ☐   TRANSPLANT ☐   DATE PLANTED: _____

SUNLIGHT EXPOSURE: SUCCESSION PLANT DATE: _____

FULL SUN ☐   PART SHADE ☐   SUCCESSION PLANT DATE: _____

PART SUN ☐   FULL SHADE ☐   SUCCESSION PLANT DATE: _____

BLOOMING DATE: DATE OF FIRST HARVEST:

HOW MUCH WATER DOES THIS PLANT NEED? _____

_____

_____

_____

HOW MUCH AND WHAT TYPE OF FERTILIZER DOES THIS PLANT NEED? _____

_____

_____

_____

WHAT PESTS OR DISEASES AFFECT THIS PLANT? _____

_____

_____

_____

_____

WHAT INSECTICIDE OR BARRIER WAS USED AND WHAT WERE THE RESULTS?

_____

_____

_____

_____

WHAT FERTILIZER WAS USED, WHEN WAS IT USED AND WHAT WERE THE
RESULTS? _____

_____

_____

_____

HOW MUCH WAS THE HARVEST? _____

_____

_____

_____

IMPORTANT TASKS/NOTES:

_____

_____

_____

_____

PLANT INFORMATION

PLANT NAME: _____   TYPE/VARIETY: _____

SEED ☐   TRANSPLANT ☐   DATE PLANTED: _____

SUNLIGHT EXPOSURE: SUCCESSION PLANT DATE: _____

FULL SUN ☐   PART SHADE ☐   SUCCESSION PLANT DATE: _____

PART SUN ☐   FULL SHADE ☐   SUCCESSION PLANT DATE: _____

BLOOMING DATE: DATE OF FIRST HARVEST:

HOW MUCH WATER DOES THIS PLANT NEED? _____

_____

_____

_____

HOW MUCH AND WHAT TYPE OF FERTILIZER DOES THIS PLANT NEED? _____

_____

_____

_____

WHAT PESTS OR DISEASES AFFECT THIS PLANT? _____

_____

_____

_____

_____

WHAT INSECTICIDE OR BARRIER WAS USED AND WHAT WERE THE RESULTS?

WHAT FERTILIZER WAS USED, WHEN WAS IT USED AND WHAT WERE THE
RESULTS?

HOW MUCH WAS THE HARVEST?

IMPORTANT TASKS/NOTES:

PLANT INFORMATION

PLANT NAME: _____   TYPE/VARIETY: _____

SEED ☐   TRANSPLANT ☐   DATE PLANTED: _____

SUNLIGHT EXPOSURE: SUCCESSION PLANT DATE: _____

FULL SUN ☐   PART SHADE ☐   SUCCESSION PLANT DATE: _____

PART SUN ☐   FULL SHADE ☐   SUCCESSION PLANT DATE: _____

BLOOMING DATE: DATE OF FIRST HARVEST:

HOW MUCH WATER DOES THIS PLANT NEED? _____

_____

_____

_____

HOW MUCH AND WHAT TYPE OF FERTILIZER DOES THIS PLANT NEED? _____

_____

_____

_____

WHAT PESTS OR DISEASES AFFECT THIS PLANT? _____

_____

_____

_____

_____

WHAT INSECTICIDE OR BARRIER WAS USED AND WHAT WERE THE RESULTS?

WHAT FERTILIZER WAS USED, WHEN WAS IT USED AND WHAT WERE THE RESULTS?

HOW MUCH WAS THE HARVEST?

IMPORTANT TASKS/NOTES:

PLANT INFORMATION

PLANT NAME: _____   TYPE/VARIETY: _____

SEED ☐   TRANSPLANT ☐   DATE PLANTED: _____

SUNLIGHT EXPOSURE: SUCCESSION PLANT DATE: _____

FULL SUN ☐   PART SHADE ☐   SUCCESSION PLANT DATE: _____

PART SUN ☐   FULL SHADE ☐   SUCCESSION PLANT DATE: _____

BLOOMING DATE: DATE OF FIRST HARVEST:

HOW MUCH WATER DOES THIS PLANT NEED? _____

_____

_____

_____

HOW MUCH AND WHAT TYPE OF FERTILIZER DOES THIS PLANT NEED? _____

_____

_____

_____

WHAT PESTS OR DISEASES AFFECT THIS PLANT? _____

_____

_____

_____

_____

WHAT INSECTICIDE OR BARRIER WAS USED AND WHAT WERE THE RESULTS?

_____

_____

_____

_____

WHAT FERTILIZER WAS USED, WHEN WAS IT USED AND WHAT WERE THE
RESULTS? _____

_____

_____

_____

HOW MUCH WAS THE HARVEST? _____

_____

_____

_____

_____

IMPORTANT TASKS/NOTES:

_____

_____

_____

PLANT INFORMATION

PLANT NAME: _____   TYPE/VARIETY: _____

SEED ☐   TRANSPLANT ☐   DATE PLANTED: _____

SUNLIGHT EXPOSURE: SUCCESSION PLANT DATE: _____

FULL SUN ☐   PART SHADE ☐   SUCCESSION PLANT DATE: _____

PART SUN ☐   FULL SHADE ☐   SUCCESSION PLANT DATE: _____

BLOOMING DATE: DATE OF FIRST HARVEST:

HOW MUCH WATER DOES THIS PLANT NEED? _____

_____

_____

HOW MUCH AND WHAT TYPE OF FERTILIZER DOES THIS PLANT NEED? _____

_____

_____

WHAT PESTS OR DISEASES AFFECT THIS PLANT? _____

_____

_____

_____

WHAT INSECTICIDE OR BARRIER WAS USED AND WHAT WERE THE RESULTS?

_____

_____

_____

_____

WHAT FERTILIZER WAS USED, WHEN WAS IT USED AND WHAT WERE THE
RESULTS? _____

_____

_____

_____

_____

HOW MUCH WAS THE HARVEST? _____

_____

_____

_____

_____

IMPORTANT TASKS/NOTES:

_____

_____

_____

_____

PLANT INFORMATION

PLANT NAME: _____   TYPE/VARIETY: _____

SEED ☐   TRANSPLANT ☐   DATE PLANTED: _____

SUNLIGHT EXPOSURE: SUCCESSION PLANT DATE: _____

FULL SUN ☐   PART SHADE ☐   SUCCESSION PLANT DATE: _____

PART SUN ☐   FULL SHADE ☐   SUCCESSION PLANT DATE: _____

BLOOMING DATE: DATE OF FIRST HARVEST:

HOW MUCH WATER DOES THIS PLANT NEED? _____

_____

_____

_____

HOW MUCH AND WHAT TYPE OF FERTILIZER DOES THIS PLANT NEED? _____

_____

_____

_____

WHAT PESTS OR DISEASES AFFECT THIS PLANT? _____

_____

_____

_____

_____

WHAT INSECTICIDE OR BARRIER WAS USED AND WHAT WERE THE RESULTS?

_____

_____

_____

_____

WHAT FERTILIZER WAS USED, WHEN WAS IT USED AND WHAT WERE THE
RESULTS? _____

_____

_____

_____

HOW MUCH WAS THE HARVEST? _____

_____

_____

_____

IMPORTANT TASKS/NOTES:
_____

_____

_____

PLANT INFORMATION

PLANT NAME: _____   TYPE/VARIETY: _____

SEED ☐   TRANSPLANT ☐   DATE PLANTED: _____

SUNLIGHT EXPOSURE: SUCCESSION PLANT DATE: _____

FULL SUN ☐   PART SHADE ☐   SUCCESSION PLANT DATE: _____

PART SUN ☐   FULL SHADE ☐   SUCCESSION PLANT DATE: _____

BLOOMING DATE: DATE OF FIRST HARVEST:

HOW MUCH WATER DOES THIS PLANT NEED? _____

_____

_____

_____

HOW MUCH AND WHAT TYPE OF FERTILIZER DOES THIS PLANT NEED? _____

_____

_____

_____

WHAT PESTS OR DISEASES AFFECT THIS PLANT? _____

_____

_____

_____

_____

WHAT INSECTICIDE OR BARRIER WAS USED AND WHAT WERE THE RESULTS?

_____

_____

_____

_____

_____

WHAT FERTILIZER WAS USED, WHEN WAS IT USED AND WHAT WERE THE
RESULTS? _____

_____

_____

_____

_____

HOW MUCH WAS THE HARVEST? _____

_____

_____

_____

_____

IMPORTANT TASKS/NOTES:

_____

_____

_____

_____

PLANT INFORMATION

PLANT NAME: _____   TYPE/VARIETY: _____

SEED ☐   TRANSPLANT ☐   DATE PLANTED: _____

SUNLIGHT EXPOSURE: SUCCESSION PLANT DATE: _____

FULL SUN ☐   PART SHADE ☐   SUCCESSION PLANT DATE: _____

PART SUN ☐   FULL SHADE ☐   SUCCESSION PLANT DATE: _____

BLOOMING DATE: DATE OF FIRST HARVEST:

HOW MUCH WATER DOES THIS PLANT NEED? _____

_____

_____

_____

HOW MUCH AND WHAT TYPE OF FERTILIZER DOES THIS PLANT NEED? _____

_____

_____

_____

WHAT PESTS OR DISEASES AFFECT THIS PLANT? _____

_____

_____

_____

_____

WHAT INSECTICIDE OR BARRIER WAS USED AND WHAT WERE THE RESULTS?

_____

_____

_____

_____

WHAT FERTILIZER WAS USED, WHEN WAS IT USED AND WHAT WERE THE
RESULTS? _____

_____

_____

_____

_____

HOW MUCH WAS THE HARVEST? _____

_____

_____

_____

_____

IMPORTANT TASKS/NOTES:

_____

_____

_____

PLANT INFORMATION

PLANT NAME: _____   TYPE/VARIETY: _____

SEED ☐   TRANSPLANT ☐   DATE PLANTED: _____

SUNLIGHT EXPOSURE: SUCCESSION PLANT DATE: _____

FULL SUN ☐   PART SHADE ☐   SUCCESSION PLANT DATE: _____

PART SUN ☐   FULL SHADE ☐   SUCCESSION PLANT DATE: _____

BLOOMING DATE: DATE OF FIRST HARVEST:

HOW MUCH WATER DOES THIS PLANT NEED? _____

_____

_____

_____

HOW MUCH AND WHAT TYPE OF FERTILIZER DOES THIS PLANT NEED? _____

_____

_____

_____

WHAT PESTS OR DISEASES AFFECT THIS PLANT? _____

_____

_____

_____

_____

WHAT INSECTICIDE OR BARRIER WAS USED AND WHAT WERE THE RESULTS?

_____

_____

_____

_____

WHAT FERTILIZER WAS USED, WHEN WAS IT USED AND WHAT WERE THE
RESULTS? _____

_____

_____

_____

_____

HOW MUCH WAS THE HARVEST? _____

_____

_____

_____

_____

IMPORTANT TASKS/NOTES:

_____

_____

_____

_____

PLANT INFORMATION

PLANT NAME: _____   TYPE/VARIETY: _____

SEED ☐   TRANSPLANT ☐   DATE PLANTED: _____

<u>SUNLIGHT EXPOSURE:</u>   SUCCESSION PLANT DATE: _____

FULL SUN ☐   PART SHADE ☐   SUCCESSION PLANT DATE: _____

PART SUN ☐   FULL SHADE ☐   SUCCESSION PLANT DATE: _____

BLOOMING DATE: DATE OF FIRST HARVEST:

HOW MUCH WATER DOES THIS PLANT NEED? _____

_____

_____

HOW MUCH AND WHAT TYPE OF FERTILIZER DOES THIS PLANT NEED? _____

_____

_____

WHAT PESTS OR DISEASES AFFECT THIS PLANT? _____

_____

_____

_____

WHAT INSECTICIDE OR BARRIER WAS USED AND WHAT WERE THE RESULTS?

_____

_____

_____

_____

WHAT FERTILIZER WAS USED, WHEN WAS IT USED AND WHAT WERE THE
RESULTS? _____

_____

_____

_____

_____

HOW MUCH WAS THE HARVEST? _____

_____

_____

_____

_____

IMPORTANT TASKS/NOTES:

_____

_____

_____

_____

PLANT INFORMATION

PLANT NAME: _____   TYPE/VARIETY: _____

SEED ☐   TRANSPLANT ☐   DATE PLANTED: _____

SUNLIGHT EXPOSURE: SUCCESSION PLANT DATE: _____

FULL SUN ☐   PART SHADE ☐   SUCCESSION PLANT DATE: _____

PART SUN ☐   FULL SHADE ☐   SUCCESSION PLANT DATE: _____

BLOOMING DATE: DATE OF FIRST HARVEST:

HOW MUCH WATER DOES THIS PLANT NEED? _____

_____

_____

_____

HOW MUCH AND WHAT TYPE OF FERTILIZER DOES THIS PLANT NEED? _____

_____

_____

_____

WHAT PESTS OR DISEASES AFFECT THIS PLANT? _____

_____

_____

_____

_____

WHAT INSECTICIDE OR BARRIER WAS USED AND WHAT WERE THE RESULTS?

_____

_____

_____

_____

WHAT FERTILIZER WAS USED, WHEN WAS IT USED AND WHAT WERE THE
RESULTS? _____

_____

_____

_____

_____

HOW MUCH WAS THE HARVEST? _____

_____

_____

_____

_____

IMPORTANT TASKS/NOTES:
_____

_____

_____

_____

PLANT INFORMATION

PLANT NAME: _____   TYPE/VARIETY: _____

SEED ☐   TRANSPLANT ☐   DATE PLANTED: _____

SUNLIGHT EXPOSURE: SUCCESSION PLANT DATE: _____

FULL SUN ☐   PART SHADE ☐   SUCCESSION PLANT DATE: _____

PART SUN ☐   FULL SHADE ☐   SUCCESSION PLANT DATE: _____

BLOOMING DATE: DATE OF FIRST HARVEST:

HOW MUCH WATER DOES THIS PLANT NEED? _____

_____

_____

_____

HOW MUCH AND WHAT TYPE OF FERTILIZER DOES THIS PLANT NEED? _____

_____

_____

_____

WHAT PESTS OR DISEASES AFFECT THIS PLANT? _____

_____

_____

_____

_____

WHAT INSECTICIDE OR BARRIER WAS USED AND WHAT WERE THE RESULTS?

_____

_____

_____

_____

WHAT FERTILIZER WAS USED, WHEN WAS IT USED AND WHAT WERE THE
RESULTS? _____

_____

_____

_____

_____

HOW MUCH WAS THE HARVEST? _____

_____

_____

_____

_____

IMPORTANT TASKS/NOTES:

_____

_____

_____

PLANT INFORMATION

PLANT NAME: _____   TYPE/VARIETY: _____

SEED ☐   TRANSPLANT ☐   DATE PLANTED: _____

SUNLIGHT EXPOSURE: SUCCESSION PLANT DATE: _____

FULL SUN ☐   PART SHADE ☐   SUCCESSION PLANT DATE: _____

PART SUN ☐   FULL SHADE ☐   SUCCESSION PLANT DATE: _____

BLOOMING DATE: DATE OF FIRST HARVEST:

HOW MUCH WATER DOES THIS PLANT NEED? _____

_____

_____

_____

HOW MUCH AND WHAT TYPE OF FERTILIZER DOES THIS PLANT NEED? _____

_____

_____

_____

WHAT PESTS OR DISEASES AFFECT THIS PLANT? _____

_____

_____

_____

_____

WHAT INSECTICIDE OR BARRIER WAS USED AND WHAT WERE THE RESULTS?

_____

_____

_____

_____

_____

WHAT FERTILIZER WAS USED, WHEN WAS IT USED AND WHAT WERE THE
RESULTS? _____

_____

_____

_____

_____

HOW MUCH WAS THE HARVEST? _____

_____

_____

_____

_____

IMPORTANT TASKS/NOTES:

_____

_____

_____

_____

PLANT INFORMATION

PLANT NAME: _____   TYPE/VARIETY: _____

SEED ☐   TRANSPLANT ☐   DATE PLANTED: _____

<u>SUNLIGHT EXPOSURE:</u>   SUCCESSION PLANT DATE: _____

FULL SUN ☐   PART SHADE ☐   SUCCESSION PLANT DATE: _____

PART SUN ☐   FULL SHADE ☐   SUCCESSION PLANT DATE: _____

BLOOMING DATE: DATE OF FIRST HARVEST:

HOW MUCH WATER DOES THIS PLANT NEED? _____

_____

_____

_____

HOW MUCH AND WHAT TYPE OF FERTILIZER DOES THIS PLANT NEED? _____

_____

_____

_____

WHAT PESTS OR DISEASES AFFECT THIS PLANT? _____

_____

_____

_____

_____

WHAT INSECTICIDE OR BARRIER WAS USED AND WHAT WERE THE RESULTS?

_____

_____

_____

_____

_____

WHAT FERTILIZER WAS USED, WHEN WAS IT USED AND WHAT WERE THE
RESULTS? _____

_____

_____

_____

_____

HOW MUCH WAS THE HARVEST? _____

_____

_____

_____

_____

IMPORTANT TASKS/NOTES:

_____

_____

_____

_____

OBSERVATIONS

WHAT PLANT WOULD YOU LIKE TO GROW AGAIN? _____

_____

_____

_____

_____

_____

_____

_____

_____

WHAT PLANTS GREW BEST IN YOUR GARDEN? _____

_____

_____

_____

_____

_____

_____

_____

_____

WHAT PLANTS DID NOT GROW WELL IN YOUR GARDEN? _____

_____

_____

_____

_____

_____

_____

_____

_____

ARE THERE ANY PESTS IN YOUR GARDEN? HOW DID YOU DEAL WITH IT?

_____

_____

_____

_____

_____

_____

_____

_____

_____

WHAT INSPIRATIONS DID YOU FIND IN YOUR GARDEN? _____

_____

_____

_____

_____

_____

_____

_____

_____

HOW WILL YOU IMPROVE YOUR GARDEN SKILLS NEXT TIME? _____

_____

_____

_____

_____

_____

_____

_____

_____

EXPENSES

QUANTITY	ITEM	COST
	TOTAL COST	

PHOTOGRAPHS

NOTES:

PHOTOGRAPHS

NOTES:

PHOTOGRAPHS

NOTES:

PHOTOGRAPHS

NOTES:

PHOTOGRAPHS

NOTES:

PHOTOGRAPHS

NOTES:

Made in the USA
Columbia, SC
31 May 2022